# Spelling One

## An Interactive Vocabulary & Spelling Workbook for 5-Year-Olds.

(With AudioBook Lessons)

By

Bukky Ekine-Ogunlana

© **Copyright Bukky Ekine-Ogunlana 2022 – All rights reserved.**

The content of this book may not be reproduced, duplicated, or transmitted without direct written permission from the author or the publisher. Under no circumstance will any blame or legal responsibility be held against the publisher, or author, for any damages, reparation, or monetary loss due to the information contained within this book. Either directly or indirectly. You are responsible for your own choices, actions, and results.

Legal Notice:
This book is copyright protected. This book is only for personal use. You cannot amend, distribute, sell, use, quote, or paraphrase any part, or the content within this book, without the consent of the author or publisher.

Disclaimer Notice:
Please note the information contained within this document is for educational and entertainment purposes only. All effort has been executed to present accurate, up-to-date, reliable, and complete information. No warranties of any kind are declared or implied. Readers acknowledge that the author is not engaging in the rendering of legal, financial, medical, or professional advice. The content within this book has been derived from various sources. Please consult a licensed professional before attempting any techniques outlined in this book.

By reading this document, the reader agrees that under no circumstances is the author responsible for any direct or indirect losses incurred as a result of the use of the information contained within this document, including, but not limited to, errors, omissions, or inaccuracies.

*Published by*
*TCEC Publishing*

# Table of Contents

Dedication ................................................................... 5

Introduction ................................................................. 6

Spelling1-1 .................................................................. 7

Spelling1-2 ................................................................. 11

Spelling1-3 ................................................................. 15

Spelling1-4 ................................................................. 19

Spelling1-5 ................................................................. 23

Spelling1-6 ................................................................. 27

Spelling1-7 ................................................................. 31

Spelling1-8 ................................................................. 35

Spelling1-9 ................................................................. 39

Spelling1-10 ............................................................... 43

Spelling1-11 ............................................................... 47

Spelling1-12 ............................................................... 51

Spelling1-13 ............................................................... 55

Spelling1-14 ............................................................... 59

Spelling1-15 ............................................................... 63

Spelling1-16 ............................................................... 67

Spelling1-17 ............................................................... 71

Spelling1-18 ............................................................... 75

Spelling1-19 ............................................................... 79

Spelling1-20 ............................................................... 83

# Table of Contents

Conclusion ....................................................................87
Answers ......................................................................89
Other Books You Love ................................................100
Audiobooks ...............................................................104
Facebook Community ................................................105
References ................................................................106

# Dedication

This book is dedicated to our three exceptional children and all the beautiful children worldwide who have passed through the T.C.E.C 6-16 years program over the years. Thank you for the opportunity to serve you and invest in your colorful and bright future.

# Introduction

Welcome to the first book of the Spelling for Kids series! This book will introduce you to practicing your spelling while enjoying it too!

It is ideal for 5-year-olds.

In Spelling One, you will learn 240 words and add them to your vocabulary. These are easy, everyday, high-frequency words we all use. Therefore, you should learn to write them down and recognize them in a sentence.

You will hear each word from the audiobook, see it written in a sentence and then write it down yourself (no cheating) to practice its dictation. Of course, you can always go back to the words you struggle with and repeat the exercise for them separately or repeat the whole chapter if necessary.

So, are you ready to thrive in spelling?

Let's begin!

# Spelling 1-1

1. Spell:

I will give you

_____ sticker

if you finish your work.

2. Spell:

_____you

want a choco cookie?

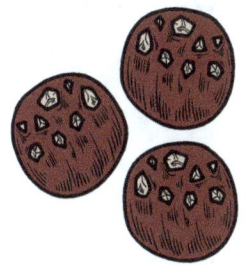

3. Spell:

Happy birthday

_____you!

# Spelling 1-1

4. Spell:
Which _____ the two is correct?

5. Spell:
Who _____I can't do it alone?

6. Spell:
Will you _____ my friend?

# Spelling 1-1

7. Spell:
Can you do _____ a favor, please?

8. Spell:
My sister is _____ year old.

9. Spell:
Do you have _____ money for ice cream?

# Spelling 1-1

10. Spell:
On your marks. Get set
_____!

11. Spell:
She went to the garden
_____ she could
play.

12. Spell:
John broke the glass
_____ accident.

That's it for lesson 1...Great work!

# Spelling 1-2

1. Spell:
Jake likes fish

_____ chips.

2. Spell:
Jude likes

_____ lollies.

3. Spell:
The _____

saves food all summer to

have for the winter.

# Spelling 1-2

4. Spell:

Drinking _____ chocolate makes me calm.

5. Spell:

John will have done his homework _____ noon.

6. Spell:

_____ on your coat, Mary; It's cold outside.

# Spelling 1-2

7. Spell:

Tigers can

_____ very fast.

8. Spell:

Jude wants to be

_____ a game

show.

9. Spell:

_____ you see

the butterfly that came

through the window?

# Spelling 1-2

10. Spell:
It's a _____ !! Congratulations on your newborn baby.

11. Spell:
_____ my point of view, what David did was wrong.

12. Spell:
The baby is sleeping in the _____.

Congrats! You have finished learning the words in lesson 2. Remember to use your dictionary to find the meaning of all the new words you have learned.

# Spelling 1-3

1. Spell:
You _____ a brave boy Adam.

2. Spell:
I went inside the house and _____ that big dog in the yard.

3. Spell:
Do _____ like vanilla ice cream?

# Spelling 1-3

4. Spell:

_____ , I like chocolate cake.

5. Spell:
The school _____ arrives every day at 7:30.

6. Spell:
_____ teacher was kind to my sister.

# Spelling 1-3

7. Spell:
I _____ for the bus in the morning.

8. Spell:
Please _____ here and wait for me.

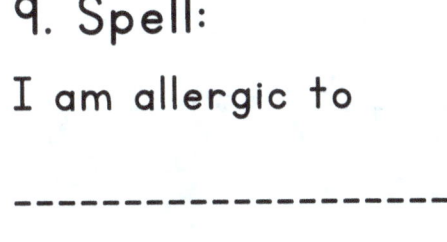

9. Spell:
I am allergic to _____.

# Spelling 1-3

10. Spell:
I had a _____ of tea with my breakfast.

11. Spell:
It is _____ birthday today.

12. Spell:
Great_____, Tom! I am proud of you!

You've made it! You completed lesson 3. Pay attention, kids; if you find it difficult to learn some words, you should write them down on paper. That will help you remember them better.

# Spelling 1-4

1. Spell:

The _____ of  England is white and red.

2. Spell:

_____ is more  clever than Mike.

3. Spell:

_____ prefer pancakes for breakfast.

# Spelling 1-4

4. Spell:
Sam hit his right

_____and could

not play in the football game.

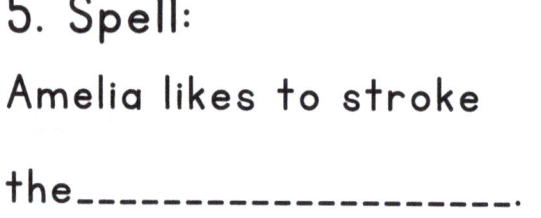

5. Spell:
Amelia likes to stroke

the_____.

6. Spell:
Going to the fairground is always

_____.

# Spelling 1-4

7. Spell:

Mathew kept his toys in the

_____ bag.

8. Spell:

_____, I will

never tell you a lie.

9. Spell:

Jack likes _____

because he is a good player.

# Spelling 1-4

10. Spell:
It was _____ older sister that taught me how to make pizza.

11. Spell:
Come on, dad; can you take _____, for pizza tonight?

12. Spell:
_____ has long blonde hair.

Great! Lesson 4 is over! I suggest you get some rest before going on to the next lesson. That will help you recharge and return to the next task more refreshed! Great work!

# Spelling 1-5

1. Spell:

My_____ is

taller than my mum.

2. Spell:

Reading a _____

is the best company.

3. Spell:

Climbing a _____

can be dangerous.

# Spelling 1-5

4. Spell:

_____,fast and don't look back!

5. Spell:
I _____ to the cinema on Saturday to watch a film.

6. Spell:
_____, I can do my work myself.

# Spelling 1-5

7. Spell:

I cannot study_____

all that noise outside.

8. Spell:

_____ sister

is five years old.

9. Spell:

The_____

constantly barks at the cat

when he sees it.

# Spelling 1-5

10. Spell:
I bought my crayon _____ the lesson.

11. Spell:
He broke the _____ of the stool.

12. Spell:
A _____ should always honor his word.

Fantastic! You have finished the words in lesson 5. What a task! Kids, keep a note: An easy way to learn the majority of new words is to break them apart; in that way, the words can be easily organized from the shortest to the longest.

# Spelling 1-6

1. Spell:
_____ favorite movie is The Beauty and the Beast.

2. Spell:
_____ the teacher politely, and she will answer your question.

3. Spell:
Have you _____ your clothes in the laundry?

# Spelling 1-6

4. Spell:
Who _____ Jude's music teacher?

5. Spell:
_____ it my turn to wash the dishes, Tom?

6. Spell:
David _____ two sisters.

# Spelling 1-6

7. Spell:

_____ are a

friendly person.

8. Spell:
He only

_____

he was sorry, and he left.

9. Spell:
It was

_____fault

that the parrot left the cage.

# Spelling 1-6

10. Spell:

_____ are coming to my party on Sunday.

11. Spell:
Where _____ you yesterday?

12. Spell:
_____ is my graduation day!

Lesson 6 has come to an end. Awesome! Keep up the excellent work! And do not forget: Repetition makes the master!

# Spelling 1-7

1. Spell:
I will _____

the sack race if I practice.

2. Spell:
Helen _____ two

brothers and a sister.

3. Spell:
There is only one

_____ in my team.

# Spelling 1-7

4. Spell:
_____ like to watch Tom and Jerry on Disney+.

5. Spell:
_____ morning to all of you!

6. Spell:
A cry for _____ was heard from down the road.

# Spelling 1-7

7. Spell:

I will invite

_____ of my

friends to my beach party.

8. Spell:

The kitchen

_____ is new.

9. Spell:

_____ you have

any pokémon stickers?

# Spelling 1-7

10. Spell:

I felt really _____ when my friend moved away from my street.

11. Spell:

Lilian wore a pretty _____ for her birthday party.

12. Spell:

A _____ is the best company for a child.

Look at how far you have gone! You have reached and completed lesson 7. What a student you are! Congratulations!

# Spelling 1-8

1. Spell:
The pig likes staying in the
_____.

2. Spell:
The farmer sold cow's
_____ to the
market.

3. Spell:
I am wearing a
_____
dress to Lucy's party.

# Spelling 1-8

4. Spell:

_____ Red Riding Hood went through the forest to visit her grandmother.

5. Spell:
Breakfast will be served _____ 8:00 am.

6. Spell:

_____ Lion King used to be one of my favorite movies.

# Spelling 1-8

7. Spell:
Can you _____

me a cup of cold water,

please?

8. Spell:
Felix did

_____

over the fence.

9. Spell:
My mum did

_____ me on

the back for being good.

# Spelling 1-8

10. Spell:
The _____ flew over my house.

11. Spell:
Mom sings a lullaby to the _____ before taking her to bed.

12. Spell:
I _____ ice cream.

Look at you! You are natural! And it seems that you will be a spelling bee master pretty soon! You have just finished lesson 8.

# Spelling 1-9

1. Spell:

In the zoo, you can also see some

_____ animals.

2. Spell:

_____ of my friends

are coming to my party.

3. Spell:

_____ of my parents

are kind to me.

# Spelling 1-9

4. Spell:
Let the _____ JESUS
come to me, said Jesus.

5. Spell:
I can _____ the apple
tree.

6. Spell:
I _____ wish he
could come to my birthday
party.

# Spelling 1-9

7. Spell:
How_____ are you?

8. Spell:
_____ people came to my birthday party.

9. Spell:
My _____ are in my cupboard.

# Spelling 1-9

10. Spell:
It's _____ outside. Why don't we light up the fireplace?

11. Spell:
_____ is the most precious material on earth.

12. Spell:
I can _____ a ball for ten minutes without it dropping.

Well done! You have finished lesson 9. You should be proud of yourself! And remember this: Always enunciate each word properly; this method will help you spell the word correctly.

# Spelling 1-10

1. Spell:
Ella walked _____ her classroom.

2. Spell:
My _____ is a police officer.

3. Spell:
I am the best student in my _____.

# Spelling 1-10

4. Spell:
Without _____,
there is no life.

5. Spell:
You have to repeat the lesson
_____ to
remember it.

6. Spell:
Cows eat
_____.

# Spelling 1-10

7. Spell:
Freddy did _____ the ball on time to Felix.

8. Spell:
Angela pulled the _____ from the soil.

9. Spell:
This _____ leads to the hidden treasure.

# Spelling 1-10

10. Spell:
Elizabeth had a _____ in the morning.

11. Spell:
An _____ is sixty minutes.

12. Spell:
Please _____ your car from here, because parking is not allowed.

*You completed lesson 10! Bravo! You are doing a great job. Pretty soon, you will be an expert in spelling.*

# Spelling 1-11

1. Spell:
Oliver was able to

_____

that the teacher was right.

2. Spell:
Nina shared

_____ of her

sausage roll with Tina.

3. Spell:

_____ is bad

for the teeth.

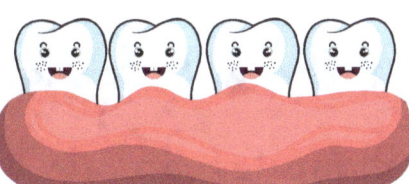

# Spelling 1-11

4. Spell:

_____ you come with me to the doctor's.

5. Spell:

_____ you like cream with your coffee?

6. Spell:
Eve is not _____ if she will attend the piano lesson.

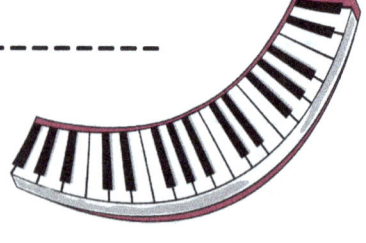

# Spelling 1-11

7. Spell:
Cameron had an operation on his right

_____

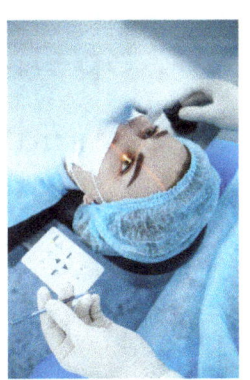

8. Spell:
You _____ always carry a painkiller with you.

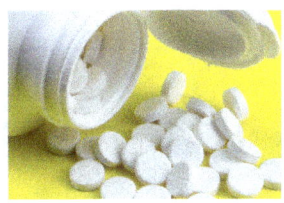

9. Spell:
_____ is going to the shopping mall on Saturday?

# Spelling 1-11

10. Spell:

The Headteacher told _____ Brown about the outing.

11. Spell:

_____. Smith is the new cook.

12. Spell:

_____ without Jack, the team won the game.

You have finished the words in lesson 11. Fantastic! Don't give up! Keep your eyes ahead to the next lesson.

# Spelling 1-12

1. Spell:
Barbie used to be my favorite
_____ when I
was a little girl.

2. Spell:
I like to push my toy
_____ .

3. Spell:
Swallows usually return to the
same site to make their
_____ each Spring.

# Spelling 1-12

4. Spell:

I have a _____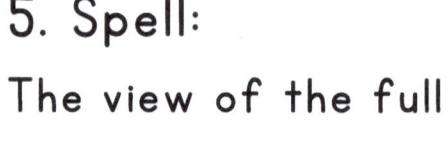

of fun storybooks at school.

5. Spell:

The view of the full

_____

by the seaside is spectacular.

6. Spell:

We _____ want

toys for our Christmas

presents.

# Spelling 1-12

7. Spell:
Driving a _____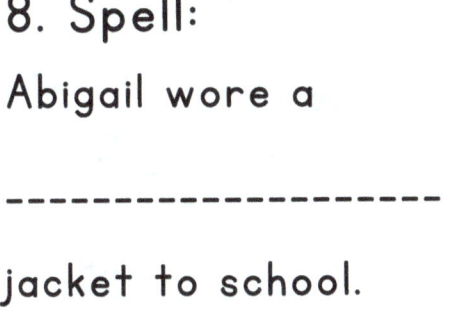
without a driving license is
dangerous and against the law.

8. Spell:
Abigail wore a

_____

jacket to school.

9. Spell:
My brother spilled his tea on
the _____.

# Spelling 1-12

10. Spell:
He arrived in the town by plane and _____  took a taxi home.

11. Spell:
_____ house has a big garden.

12. Spell:
I am an only _____ .

> You have done a great job finishing words in lesson 12. With this rhythm, you are about to be a master in spelling soon.

# Spelling 1-13

1. Spell:
My_____ has three bedrooms.

2. Spell:
We should knock on the _____ before we enter a room.

3. Spell:
My mother always gives a penny to the _____ man outside the church.

# Spelling 1-13

4. Spell:
Did you _____ 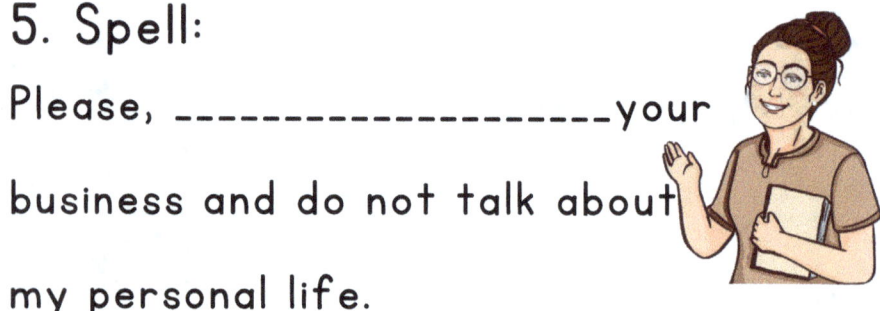 your car keys?

5. Spell:
Please, _____ your 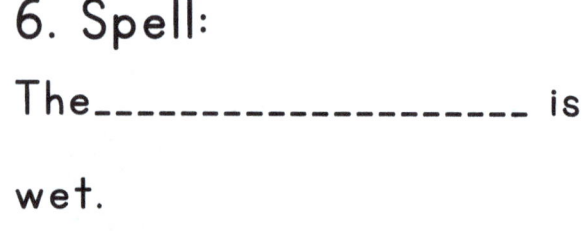 business and do not talk about my personal life.

6. Spell:
The_____ is  wet.

# Spelling 1-13

7. Spell:

I am going home

_____ I am tired.

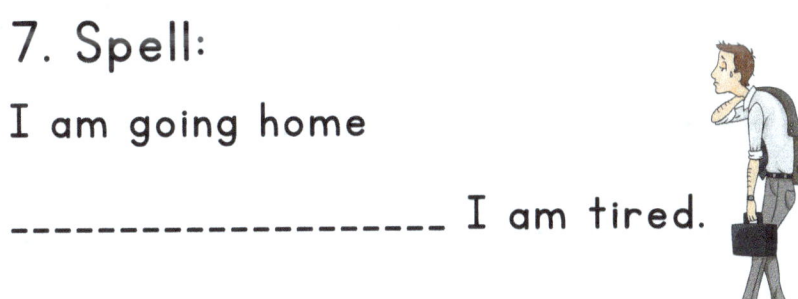

8. Spell:

Julia is always _____

to me.

9. Spell:

I am standing

_____ the tree.

# Spelling 1-13

10. Spell:
I have not seen a bigger boat in my _____ life.

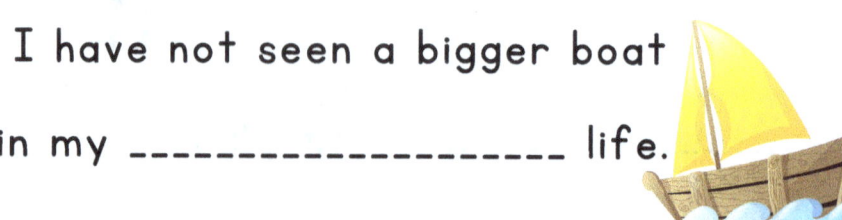

11. Spell:
She _____ off the chair.

12. Spell:
Tim _____ hay fever and should go to the doctor.

> Congrats! You have made such Progress! You finished the words in lesson 13 already. Don't forget to practice new vocabulary every week. First, learn the meaning of the word and the spelling of it. Then surprise everyone with your spelling skills.

# Spelling 1-14

1. Spell:
I _____ you I would do my homework when I finished eating.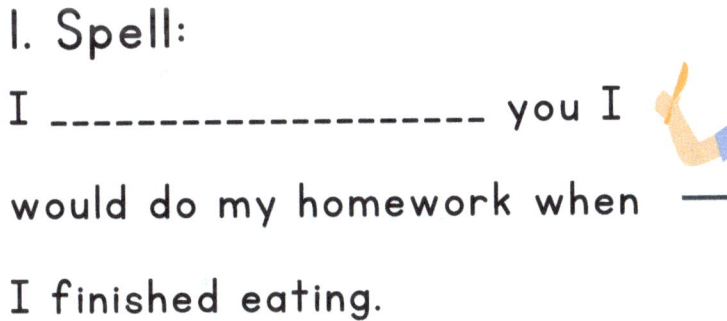

2. Spell:
_____ girl in my class is intelligent.

3. Spell:
_____ news! John passed the exam!

# Spelling 1-14

4. Spell:
I made a promise, and I will not _____ it.

5. Spell:
I like eating _____ with my fries.

6. Spell:
My mum is always _____ with her work.

# Spelling 1-14

7. Spell:
Many _____ are coming to watch the match.

8. Spell:
Sandra is a _____ girl.

9. Spell:
Helen is a _____ girl.

# Spelling 1-14

10. Spell:

I will come to your house

_____ school

today.

11. Spell:

I am very _____

at running 100 metres sprints.

12. Spell:

My team came _____

in the game.

*What progress! You completed lesson 14 already. You should be proud of yourself!*

# Spelling 1-15

1. Spell:
You should better leave the _____ behind and go on with your life.

2. Spell:
My_____ is a police officer.

3. Spell:
My_____ is fun because of my fantastic teacher.

# Spelling 1-15

4. Spell:

Planet earth consists of 75%

_____ .

5. Spell:

Kate, please do not be so late to return to the house _____

6. Spell:

The _____ is green.

# Spelling 1-15

7. Spell:
If you _____ the exams, I will buy you a tablet.

8. Spell:
You must water the _____ for it to grow.

9. Spell:
Every _____ from this point leads to the lake.

# spelling 1-15

10. Spell:
Elizabeth had a _____
in the morning.

11. Spell:
The bus takes an _____
to arrive at school.

12. Spell:
My teacher will _____
Ella from my class next term.

Wonderful! You have completed words in lesson 15. Keep up the excellent work, and don't forget: Words matter, and most importantly, correctly written words matter.

# Spelling 1-16

1. Spell:
This silk shirt is so

_____.

2. Spell:
I walked _____

the road to meet my dad.

3. Spell:
My sister can _____

a house.

# Spelling 1-16

4. Spell:
There is no _____
here for more toys.

5. Spell:
Jude plays the
_____ at church.

6. Spell:
Ethan sits at the
_____ of the
class.

# Spelling 1-16

7. Spell:
The _____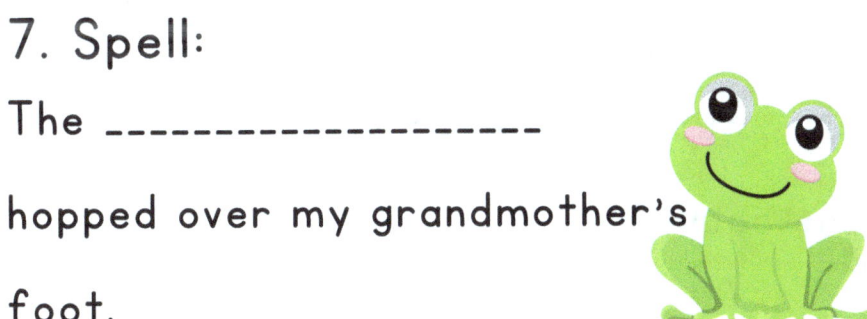
hopped over my grandmother's
foot.

8. Spell:
_____, sweet
_____, said mom
after returning from vacation.

9. Spell:
Mrs. Jones took
_____ for a
swimming lesson.

# spelling 1-16

10. Spell:
She is so talented at singing that she could become a shining _____.

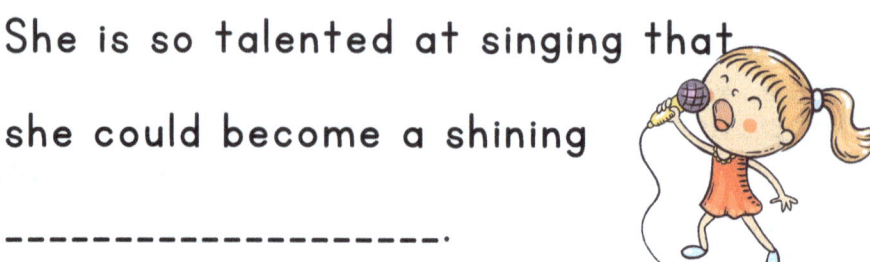

11. Spell:
Oh _____! I think I lost my wallet!

12. Spell:
I am _____ going to the football match today.

You're almost finished with becoming a spelling master. You are doing so well! You have completed words in spelling lesson 16. Bravo!

# Spelling 1-17

1. Spell:

 Ella _____

long black hair.

2. Spell:

 I will come to your house

 _____ you

invite me.

3. Spell:

My dad put the fish in the

_____.

# Spelling 1-17

4. Spell:
The _____ are coming to repair my house.

5. Spell:
The _____ apple was thrown away.

6. Spell:
Bella will _____ me up after school.

# Spelling 1-17

7. Spell:
We ate hotdogs after the movie was _____.

8. Spell:
How _____ your trip to the Bahamas?

9. Spell:
Every Christmas, I _____ Christmas card to my grandparents.

# Spelling 1-17

10. Spell:
The black _____ is under my bed.

11. Spell:
I learned to _____ in the pool.

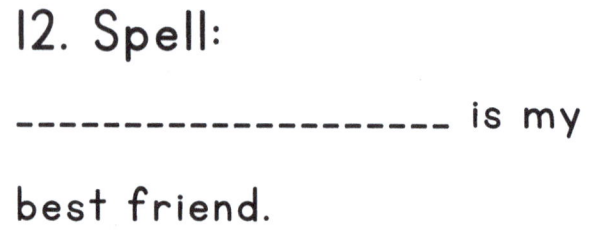

12. Spell:
_____ is my best friend.

> Fantastic! You have completed lesson 17! You're almost done. Don't quit now! You are close to the end.

# Spelling 1-18

1. Spell:
My _____ is coming to my party.

2. Spell:
I like my _____.

3. Spell:
I was _____ a toddler.

# Spelling 1-18

4. Spell:

_____on, mom! Why can't I play a little more with the tablet?

5. Spell:

_____ of my books are in the bookcase.

6. Spell:

_____ you are; I have been looking everywhere for you!

# Spelling 1-18

7. Spell:

_____ are seven days in a week.

8. Spell:

_____ are you going on Saturday?

9. Spell:
I _____ dancing.

# Spelling 1-18

10. Spell:

I can _____ the trolley.

11. Spell:

I can _____ the rope.

12. Spell:

 My cup is _____ of water.

Spelling lesson 18 is over! You finished it and, more importantly, learned the lesson's words. However, if you have doubts about one or more words, do not worry; return to it and make as many revisions as necessary.

# Spelling 1-19

1. Spell:
The _____ is on the sea.

2. Spell:
John proposed to Mary with a diamond _____ .

3. Spell:
Ok, Mark, I'll _____ you tonight at the cinema.

# Spelling 1-19

4. Spell:

I got a new _____

for my birthday.

5. Spell:

_____ is six

years older than his sister.

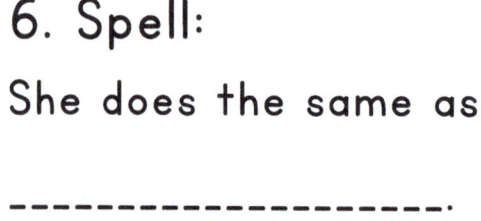

6. Spell:

She does the same as

_____.

# Spelling 1-19

7. Spell:
The chips were

_____ and crispy.

8. Spell:
Let's _____

this exercise and go to the

next one.

9. Spell:
I am going to my _____

lesson on Friday.

# Spelling 1-19

10. Spell:

My best _____ is rice with chicken.

11. Spell:

_____ you seen my glasses?

12. Spell:

Helen was a _____ friend to my little brother when he was sad.

*Excellent work, kid! You have made it! You are so close to the end. Lesson 19 is complete. One more task is left, and you are done with Spelling one. Right? Okay, let's go!*

# Spelling 1-20

1. Spell:
Dorothy has a

_____ dolly.

2. Spell:
Emily will _____

at it later today.

3. Spell:
Children should not take their heads

out of the car

_____ .

# Spelling 1-20

4. Spell:

I will take the test on the last

_____ of school.

5. Spell:

The country's young

_____ joined the

army and went to war.

6. Spell:

I had a restful _____

yesterday.

# Spelling 1-20

7. Spell:
I met a nice _____ at the bus stop today.

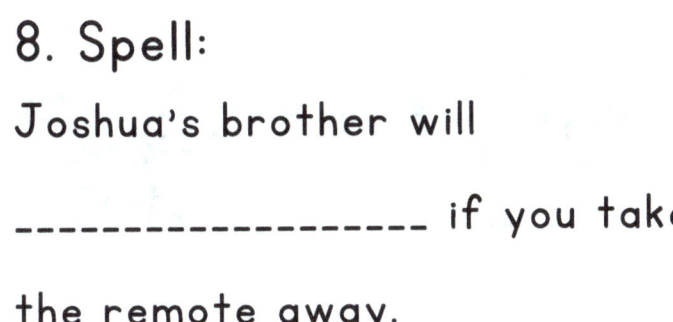

8. Spell:
Joshua's brother will _____ if you take the remote away.

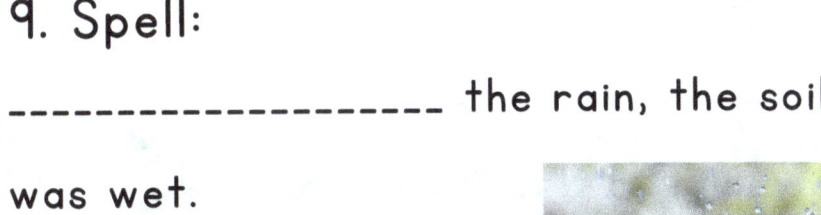

9. Spell:
_____ the rain, the soil was wet.

# Spelling 1-20

10. Spell:
Going to _____ makes you learn new things and meet new friends.

11. Spell:
The radio plays my favorite _____.

12. Spell:
My _____ are traveling to New York next week.

Congrats! You have finished learning the words in spelling one.

# Conclusion

CONGRATULATIONS, you little spelling heroes!

You have arrived at the end of Spelling 1! You have made it, and you should be proud of yourself ! Now you can give yourself a round of applause for getting this far.

I hope that finishing Spelling 1 has boosted your confidence in your vocabulary knowledge and your spelling kills with 240 words.

However, if you got some words incorrect, no worries; we all learn at different paces and in our own time. No judgement here. To improve your "weak spots", you can always return to and revise the words you found the hardest to grasp and have another look at their spelling or try to remember their meaning.

And don't forget that repeating the words you got wrong about 5 times can bring you back to the masters level and prepare you for the next challenge!

So, that's it folks!
See you in Spelling 2

# Please leave a 1-click Review!

I would be incredibly thankful if you could take just 60 seconds to write a brief review on Amazon or the platform of purchase, even if it's just a few sentences!

# Answers

## Spelling 1-1

1. Spell: <u>A</u>
2. Spell: <u>Do</u>
3. Spell: <u>To</u>
4. Spell: <u>Of</u>
5. Spell: <u>Says</u>
6. Spell: <u>Be</u>
7. Spell: <u>Me</u>
8. Spell: <u>One</u>
9. Spell: <u>Any</u>
10. Spell: <u>Go</u>
11. Spell: <u>So</u>
12. Spell: <u>By</u>

## Spelling 1-2

1. Spell: <u>And</u>
2. Spell: <u>Big</u>
3. Spell: <u>Ant</u>
4. Spell: <u>Hot</u>
5. Spell: <u>By</u>
6. Spell: <u>Put</u>
7. Spell: <u>Run</u>
8. Spell: <u>On</u>
9. Spell: <u>Did</u>
10. Spell: <u>Boy</u>
11. Spell: <u>From</u>
12. Spell: <u>Cot</u>

# Answers

## Spelling 1-3

1. Spell: Are
2. Spell: Saw
3. Spell: You
4. Spell: Yes
5. Spell: Bus
6. Spell: The
7. Spell: Ran
8. Spell: Sit
9. Spell: Nuts
10. Spell: Cup
11. Spell: Her
12. Spell: Job

## Spelling 1-4

1. Spell: Flag
2. Spell: He
3. Spell: We
4. Spell: Leg
5. Spell: Cow
6. Spell: Fun
7. Spell: Big
8. Spell: No
9. Spell: Him
10. Spell: His
11. Spell: Us
12. Spell: She

# Answers

## Spelling 1-5

1. Spell: <u>Dad</u>
2. Spell: <u>Book</u>
3. Spell: <u>Tree</u>
4. Spell: <u>Run</u>
5. Spell: <u>Went</u>
6. Spell: <u>Yes</u>
7. Spell: <u>With</u>
8. Spell: <u>My</u>
9. Spell: <u>Dog</u>
10. Spell: <u>For</u>
11. Spell: <u>Leg</u>
12. Spell: <u>Man</u>

## Spelling 1-6

1. Spell: <u>My</u>
2. Spell: <u>Ask</u>
3. Spell: <u>Put</u>
4. Spell: <u>Was</u>
5. Spell: <u>Is</u>
6. Spell: <u>Has</u>
7. Spell: <u>You</u>
8. Spell: <u>Said</u>
9. Spell: <u>Your</u>
10. Spell: <u>They</u>
11. Spell: <u>Were</u>
12. Spell: <u>Today</u>

# Answers

## Spelling 1-7

1. Spell: <u>Win</u>
2. Spell: <u>Has</u>
3. Spell: <u>Girl</u>
4. Spell: <u>I</u>
5. Spell: <u>Good</u>
6. Spell: <u>Help</u>
7. Spell: <u>Six</u>
8. Spell: <u>Tap</u>
9. Spell: <u>Do</u>
10. Spell: <u>Sad</u>
11. Spell: <u>Dress</u>
12. Spell: <u>Pet</u>

## Spelling 1-8

1. Spell: <u>Mud</u>
2. Spell: <u>Milk</u>
3. Spell: <u>Red</u>
4. Spell: <u>Little</u>
5. Spell: <u>At</u>
6. Spell: <u>The</u>
7. Spell: <u>Get</u>
8. Spell: <u>Jump</u>
9. Spell: <u>Pat</u>
10. Spell: <u>Bird</u>
11. Spell: <u>Baby</u>
12. Spell: <u>Like</u>

# Answers

## Spelling 1-9

1. Spell: <u>Wild</u>
2. Spell: <u>Most</u>
3. Spell: <u>Both</u>
4. Spell: <u>Children</u>
5. Spell: <u>Climb</u>
6. Spell: <u>Only</u>
7. Spell: <u>Old</u>
8. Spell: <u>Many</u>
9. Spell: <u>Clothes</u>
10. Spell: <u>Cold</u>
11. Spell: <u>Gold</u>
12. Spell: <u>Hold</u>

## Spelling 1-10

1. Spell: <u>Past</u>
2. Spell: <u>Father</u>
3. Spell: <u>Class</u>
4. Spell: <u>Water</u>
5. Spell: <u>Again</u>
6. Spell: <u>Grass</u>
7. Spell: <u>Pass</u>
8. Spell: <u>Plant</u>
9. Spell: <u>Path</u>
10. Spell: <u>Bath</u>
11. Spell: <u>Hour</u>
12. Spell: <u>Move</u>

# Answers

## Spelling 1-11

1. Spell: <u>Prove</u>
2. Spell: <u>Half</u>
3. Spell: <u>Sugar</u>
4. Spell: <u>Could</u>
5. Spell: <u>Would</u>
6. Spell: <u>Sure</u>
7. Spell: <u>Eve</u>
8. Spell: <u>Should</u>
9. Spell: <u>Who</u>
10. Spell: <u>Mr</u>
11. Spell: <u>Mrs</u>
12. Spell: <u>Even</u>

## Spelling 1-12

1. Spell: <u>Doll</u>
2. Spell: <u>Pram</u>
3. Spell: <u>Nest</u>
4. Spell: <u>Lot</u>
5. Spell: <u>Moon</u>
6. Spell: <u>All</u>
7. Spell: <u>Car</u>
8. Spell: <u>Red</u>
9. Spell: <u>Rug</u>
10. Spell: <u>Then</u>
11. Spell: <u>Our</u>
12. Spell: <u>Child</u>

# Answers

## Spelling 1-13

1. Spell: <u>Prove</u>
2. Spell: <u>Half</u>
3. Spell: <u>Sugar</u>
4. Spell: <u>Could</u>
5. Spell: <u>Would</u>
6. Spell: <u>Sure</u>
7. Spell: <u>Eve</u>
8. Spell: <u>Should</u>
9. Spell: <u>Who</u>
10. Spell: <u>Mr</u>
11. Spell: <u>Mrs</u>
12. Spell: <u>Even</u>

## Spelling 1-14

1. Spell: <u>Told</u>
2. Spell: <u>Every</u>
3. Spell: <u>Great</u>
4. Spell: <u>Break</u>
5. Spell: <u>Steak</u>
6. Spell: <u>Busy</u>
7. Spell: <u>People</u>
8. Spell: <u>Pretty</u>
9. Spell: <u>Beautiful</u>
10. Spell: <u>After</u>
11. Spell: <u>Fast</u>
12. Spell: <u>Last</u>

# Answers

## Spelling 1-15

1. Spell: <u>Past</u>
2. Spell: <u>Father</u>
3. Spell: <u>Class</u>
4. Spell: <u>Water</u>
5. Spell: <u>Again</u>
6. Spell: <u>Grass</u>
7. Spell: <u>Pass</u>
8. Spell: <u>Plant</u>
9. Spell: <u>Path</u>
10. Spell: <u>Bath</u>
11. Spell: <u>Hour</u>
12. Spell: <u>Move</u>

## Spelling 1-16

1. Spell: <u>Soft</u>
2. Spell: <u>Down</u>
3. Spell: <u>Draw</u>
4. Spell: <u>Room</u>
5. Spell: <u>Drum</u>
6. Spell: <u>Back</u>
7. Spell: <u>Frog</u>
8. Spell: <u>Home</u>
9. Spell: <u>Them</u>
10. Spell: <u>Star</u>
11. Spell: <u>Boy</u>
12. Spell: <u>Not</u>

# Answers

## Spelling 1-17

1. Spell: <u>Has</u>
2. Spell: <u>If</u>
3. Spell: <u>Pond</u>
4. Spell: <u>Men</u>
5. Spell: <u>Bad</u>
6. Spell: <u>Pick</u>
7. Spell: <u>Over</u>
8. Spell: <u>Was</u>
9. Spell: <u>Send</u>
10. Spell: <u>Box</u>
11. Spell: <u>Swim</u>
12. Spell: <u>She</u>

## Spelling 1-18

1. Spell: <u>Friend</u>
2. Spell: <u>School</u>
3. Spell: <u>Once</u>
4. Spell: <u>Come</u>
5. Spell: <u>Some</u>
6. Spell: <u>Here</u>
7. Spell: <u>There</u>
8. Spell: <u>Where</u>
9. Spell: <u>Love</u>
10. Spell: <u>Push</u>
11. Spell: <u>Pull</u>
12. Spell: <u>Full</u>

# Answers

## Spelling 1-19

1. Spell: <u>Ship</u>
2. Spell: <u>Ring</u>
3. Spell: <u>See</u>
4. Spell: <u>Dress</u>
5. Spell: <u>He</u>
6. Spell: <u>Me</u>
7. Spell: <u>Thin</u>
8. Spell: <u>Skip</u>
9. Spell: <u>Drum</u>
10. Spell: <u>Food</u>
11. Spell: <u>Have</u>
12. Spell: <u>Good</u>

## Spelling 1-20

1. Spell: <u>Pretty</u>
2. Spell: <u>Look</u>
3. Spell: <u>Window</u>
4. Spell: <u>Day</u>
5. Spell: <u>Men</u>
6. Spell: <u>Sleep</u>
7. Spell: <u>Lady</u>
8. Spell: <u>Cry</u>
9. Spell: <u>After</u>
10. Spell: <u>School</u>
11. Spell: <u>Song</u>
12. Spell: <u>Parents</u>

Spelling One is an essential tool for children and young adults, along with some unique categories for students and teachers, in learning correct pronunciation and orthography.

Still, the work remains in the hands of parents, tutors and children to make the most of this book. The energy and time you put into the exercise of each unit will determine your success.

Parents, assist your children on their learning journey. Teachers complement your school lesson with this spelling manual. And kids take the initiative to improve your language so that you will ensure your ticket to proceed in your studies and your life.

This book will be your helping hand. Read it, revise it, and you will gain an extra asset. The guide will add additional value to our educational system, fight illiteracy, and enhance children's learning processes.

Thank you for purchasing Spelling One

# Other Books You'll Love!

1. **Spelling one: An Interactive Vocabulary & Spelling**
   Workbook for 5-Year-Olds. *(With Audiobook Lessons)*

2. **Spelling Two: An Interactive Vocabulary & Spelling**
   Workbook for 6-Year-Olds. *(With Audiobook Lessons)*

3. **Spelling Three: An Interactive Vocabulary & Spelling**
   Workbook for 7-Year-Olds. *(With Audiobook Lessons)*

4. **Spelling Four: An Interactive Vocabulary & Spelling**
   Workbook for 8-Year-Olds. *(With Audiobook Lessons)*

5. **Spelling Five: An Interactive Vocabulary & Spelling**
   Workbook for 9-Year-Olds. *(With Audiobook Lessons)*

6. **Spelling Six: An Interactive Vocabulary & Spelling**
   Workbook for 10 & 11 Years Old. *(With Audiobook Lessons)*

7. **Spelling Seven: An Interactive Vocabulary & Spelling**
   Workbook for 12-14 Years-Old. *(With Audiobook Lessons)*

# Other Books You'll Love!

8. **Raising Boys in Today's Digital World:**
Proven Positive Parenting Tips for Raising Respectful, Successful, and Confident Boys

9. **Raising Girls in Today's Digital World:**
Proven Positive Parenting Tips for Raising Respectful, Successful, and Confident Girls

10. **Raising Kids in Today's Digital World:**
Proven Positive Parenting Tips for Raising Respectful, Successful, and Confident Kids

11. **The Child Development and Positive Parenting Master Class 2-in-1 Bundle:**
Proven Methods for Raising Well-Behaved and Intelligent Children, with Accelerated Learning Methods

12. **Parenting Teens in Today's Challenging World 2-in-1 Bundle:**
Proven Methods for Improving Teenager's Behaviour with Positive Parenting and Family Communication

13. **Life Strategies for Teenagers:**
Positive Parenting, Tips and Understanding Teens for Better Communication and a Happy Family

14. **Parenting Teen Girls in Today's Challenging World:**
Proven Methods for Improving Teenager's Behaviour with Whole Brain Training

# Other Books You'll Love!

15. **Parenting Teen Boys in Today's Challenging World:** Proven Methods for Improving Teenager's Behaviour with Whole Brain Training

16. **101 Tips For Helping With Your Child's Learning**: Proven Strategies for Accelerated Learning and Raising Smart Children Using Positive Parenting Skills

17. **101 Tips for Child Development:** Proven Methods for Raising Children and Improving Kids Behavior with Whole Brain Training

18. **Financial Tips to Help Kids:** Proven Methods for Teaching Kids Money Management and Financial Responsibility

19. **Healthy Habits for Kids:** Positive Parenting Tips for Fun Kids Exercises, Healthy Snacks, and Improved Kids Nutrition

20. **Mini Habits for Happy Kids:** Proven Parenting Tips for Positive Discipline and Improving Kids' Behavior

21. **Good Habits for Healthy Kids 2-in-1 Combo Pack**: Proven Positive Parenting Tips for Improving Kid's Fitness and Children's Behavior

22. T Raising Teenagers to Choose Wisely: Keeping your Teen Secure in a Big World

23. **Tips for #CollegeLife:** Powerful College Advice for Excelling as a College Freshman

# Other Books You'll Love!

24. **The Career Success Formula:**
Proven Career Development Advice and Finding Rewarding Employment for Young Adults and College Graduates

25. **The Motivated Young Adult's Guide to Career Success and Adulthood:**
Proven Tips for Becoming a Mature Adult, Starting a Rewarding Career, and Finding Life Balance

26. **Bedtime Stories for Kids:**
Short Funny Stories and poems Collection for Children and Toddlers

27. **Guide for Boarding School Life**

28. **The Fear of The Lord:**
How God's Honour Guarantees Your Peace

# Audiobooks

Are available at any of the following retailers:

**1. Kobo**
https://www.kobo.com/us/en/audiobook/spelling-one

**2. Google Store**
https://play.google.com/store/audiobooks/details/Bukky_Ekine_Ogunlana_Spelling_One?id=AQAAAEAi4SuhGM

**3. Libro**
https://libro.fm/audiobooks/9798368929880

**4. Storytel**
https://www.storytel.com/se/sv/books/4028820

**5. Scribd**
https://www.scribd.com/audiobook/631546677/Spelling-One-An-Interactive-Vocabulary-and-Spelling-Workbook-for-5-Year-Olds-With-AudioBook-Lessons

**6. Audiobooks**
https://www.audiobooks.com/audiobook/spelling-one-an-interactive-vocabulary-and-spelling-workbook-for-5-year-olds-with-audiobook-lessons/674795

**7. Barnes and Noble**
https://www.barnesandnoble.com/w/spelling-one-bukky-ekine-ogunlana/1143208355

**8. Spotify**
https://open.spotify.com/show/3u5811rG2LFRokWB710ekX

And all other audiobook retailers!

# Facebook Community

I invite you to our Facebook community group to visit this link and simply click the join group.

**https://www.facebook.com/groups/397683731371863**

This is a private group where parents, teachers, and carers can learn, share tips, ask questions, and discuss and get valuable content about raising and parenting modern children.

It is a very supportive and encouraging group where valuable content, free resources, and exciting discussion about parenting are shared. You can use this to benefit from social media.

You will learn a lot from schoolteachers, experts, counselors, and new and experienced parents, and stay updated with our latest releases.

See you there!

# References

[1] https://www.theseus.fi/bitstream/handle/10024/50239/Anttila_Marianna_Saikkonen_Pinja.pdf

[2] https://www.researchgate.net/publication/283721084_Early_Reading_Development

[3] https://www2.ed.gov/parents/academic/help/adolescence/adolescence.pdf

[4] http://centerforchildwelfare.org/kb/prprouthome/Helping%20Your%20Children%20Navigate%20Their%20Teenage%20Years.pdf

[5] https://www.childrensmn.org/images/family_resource_pdf/027121.pdf

[6] https://educationnorthwest.org/sites/default/files/developing-empathy-in-children--and-youth.pdf

[7] https://www.researchgate.net/publication/263227023_Family_Time_Activities_and_Adolescents'_Emotional_Well-being

[8] http://www.delmarlearning.com/companions/content/1418019224/AdditionalSupport/box11.1.pdf

[9] https://exeter.anglican.org/wp-content/uploads/2014/11/Listening-to-children-leaflet_NCB.pdf

[10] https://www.researchgate.net/publication/312600262_Creative_Thinking_among_Preschool_Children

www.ingramcontent.com/pod-product-compliance
Lightning Source LLC
Chambersburg PA
CBHW050302120526
44590CB00016B/2458